By Laura Williams
Translated by Emma Svensson

© 2022 Williams Books
1 rue de l'église, 91430 Igny
Dépôt légal : Décembre 2022
ISBN 978-2-494614-52-9
Imprimé à la demande par Amazon
Loi n° 49-956 du 16 juillet 1949 sur les publications destinées à la jeunesse

att sova

to sleep

att ta ett bad

to take a bath

att krypa

to crawl

att spela

to play

att sitta

to sit

att gråta

to cry

att stå

to stand

att klappa

to clap

att läsa

to read

att äta

to eat

att dricka

to drink

att skratta

to laugh

att krama

to hug

att gå

to walk

att springa

to run

att kyssa

to kiss

att hoppa

to jump

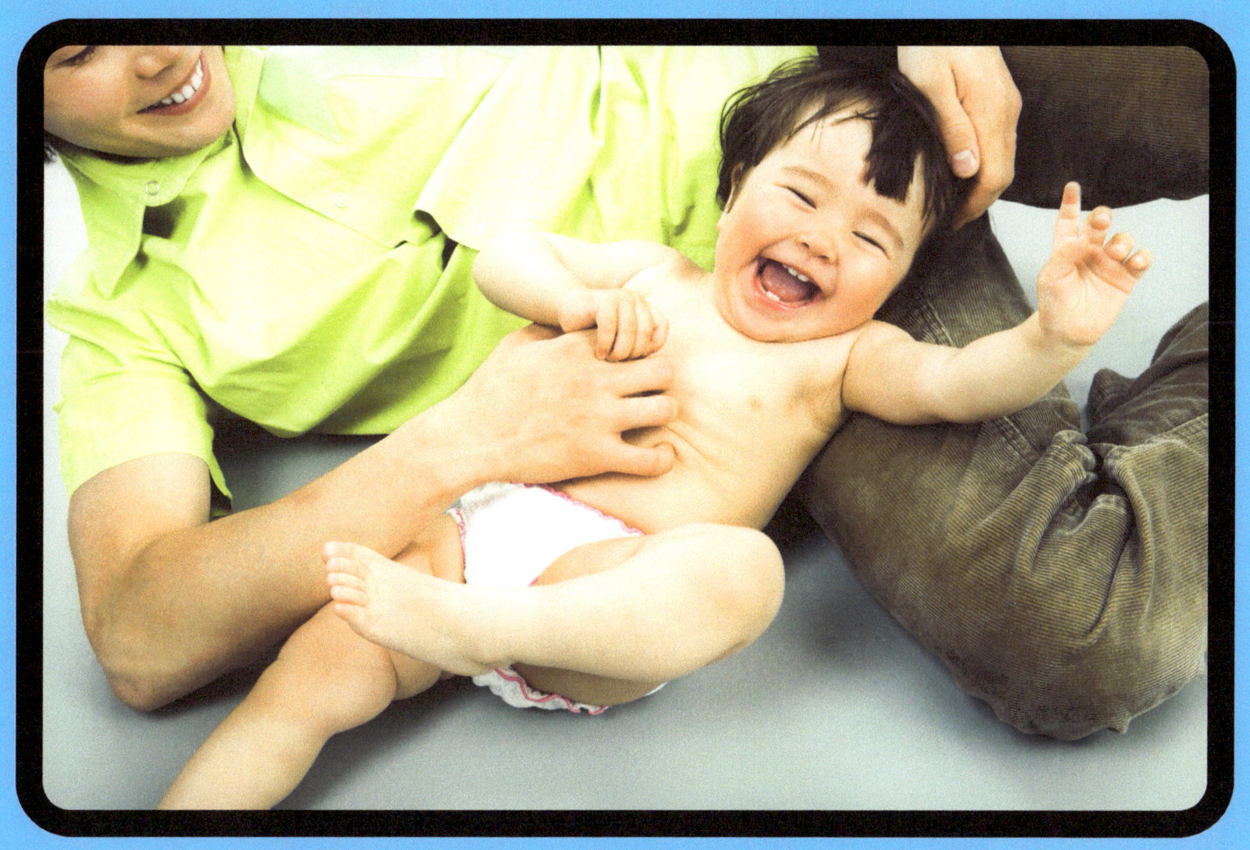

att kittla

to tickle

att dansa

to dance

att laga mat

to cook

att knäböja

to kneel

att trycka

to push

att dra

to pull

att skriva

to write

att sjunga

to sing

Thank you

Thank you for purchasing "Swedish-English Words for Toddlers"! Your support means a lot to me, and I hope you and your child enjoy these books.

If you have a moment, I would greatly appreciate it if you could leave a review on Amazon. Your feedback will help me improve future editions of the series and create more resources for bilingual children.

Thank you again for your support. You can access the reviews on Amazon by scanning the QR code below or by visiting the link below:

https://www.amazon.com/review/create-review?&asin=249461452X

Thank you for helping me continue my work as a language teacher and translator. Your support is greatly appreciated!

In the same collection

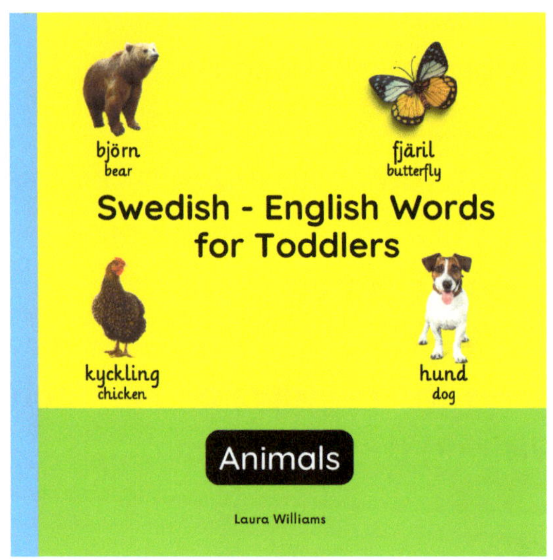

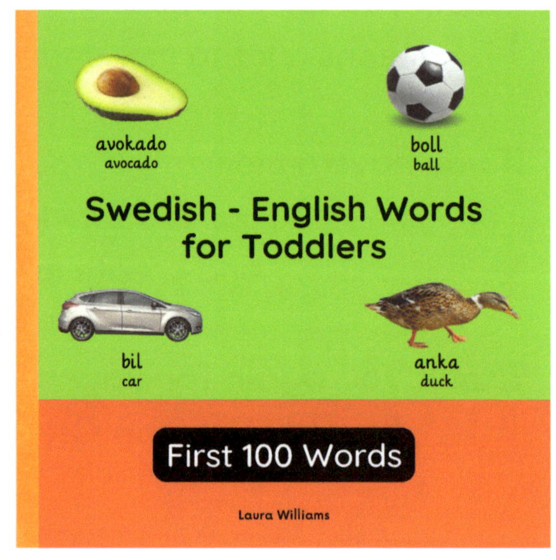